PISCES SUN

SYMBOL: FISHES / ELEMENT: WATER / RULING PLANET: NEPTUNE / POWER COLOR: AQUAMARINE

February 19 – March 20

Shonette Charles

Copyright © 2023 by Shonette Charles.

All rights reserved. No part of this publication may be reproduced, distributed, or transmitted in any form or by any means, including photocopying, recording, or other electronic or mechanical methods, without the prior written permission of the publisher, except in the case of brief quotations embodied in critical reviews and certain other noncommercial uses permitted by copyright law. For permission requests, write to the publisher.

Seamare Press LLC
PO Box 99095
Raleigh, NC 27624
www.seamarepress.com

Quantity sales. Special discounts are available on quantity purchases by corporations, associations, and others. For details, contact the address above.

Pisces Sun Vibes / Shonette Charles. — 1st ed.
ISBN 978-1-955689-32-8

Published in the United States of America by Seamare Press, Raleigh, NC.

YOUR ENERGY FIELDS

The human energy field is a complex and dynamic system of energy that surrounds and permeates our physical body. It is made up of several different layers, each of which corresponds to different aspects of our being. Understanding the different layers of the human energy field and how they work can help us to develop greater awareness and sensitivity to the subtle energies that shape our reality.

PHYSICAL
The most dense and tangible layer. It is closely connected to the physical body and is responsible for the overall health and vitality of the body. Influenced by nutrition, exercise, and environmental toxins.

ETHERIC
Subtle and dynamic, it surrounds and interpenetrates the physical layer and is responsible for the vital life force energy that animates the body. Influenced by stress, trauma, and energy blockages.

EMOTIONAL
Dynamic and ever-changing layer. It is closely connected to our emotional experiences and patterns, and responsible for the energy of our emotions. Influenced by emotional trauma, repressed emotions, and emotional expression.

MENTAL
Complex and abstract layer. It is closely connected to our thoughts and beliefs and responsible for the energy of our mental processes. Influenced by limiting beliefs, negative self-talk, and mental clarity.

SPIRITUAL
The most expansive and subtle layer. It is closely connected to our spiritual practices and beliefs and responsible for the energy of our spiritual experiences. Influenced by meditation, prayer, and connection to a higher power.

Conscious vs Subconscious

While the conscious and the subconscious are distinct aspects of our mental processes, they are also interconnected and can influence each other in complex ways. For example, our subconscious beliefs and desires can influence our conscious thoughts and actions, while our conscious experiences can shape our subconscious processing and perception of the world.

- Awareness: Mental processes that are not immediately accessible to our conscious awareness
- Control: Operates outside of our conscious control and can influence our behavior in ways that we may not be aware of
- Processing: Automatic and passive processing of information
- Capacity: Greater capacity for processing and storing information
- Will: Can operate independently of our conscious intentions and desires

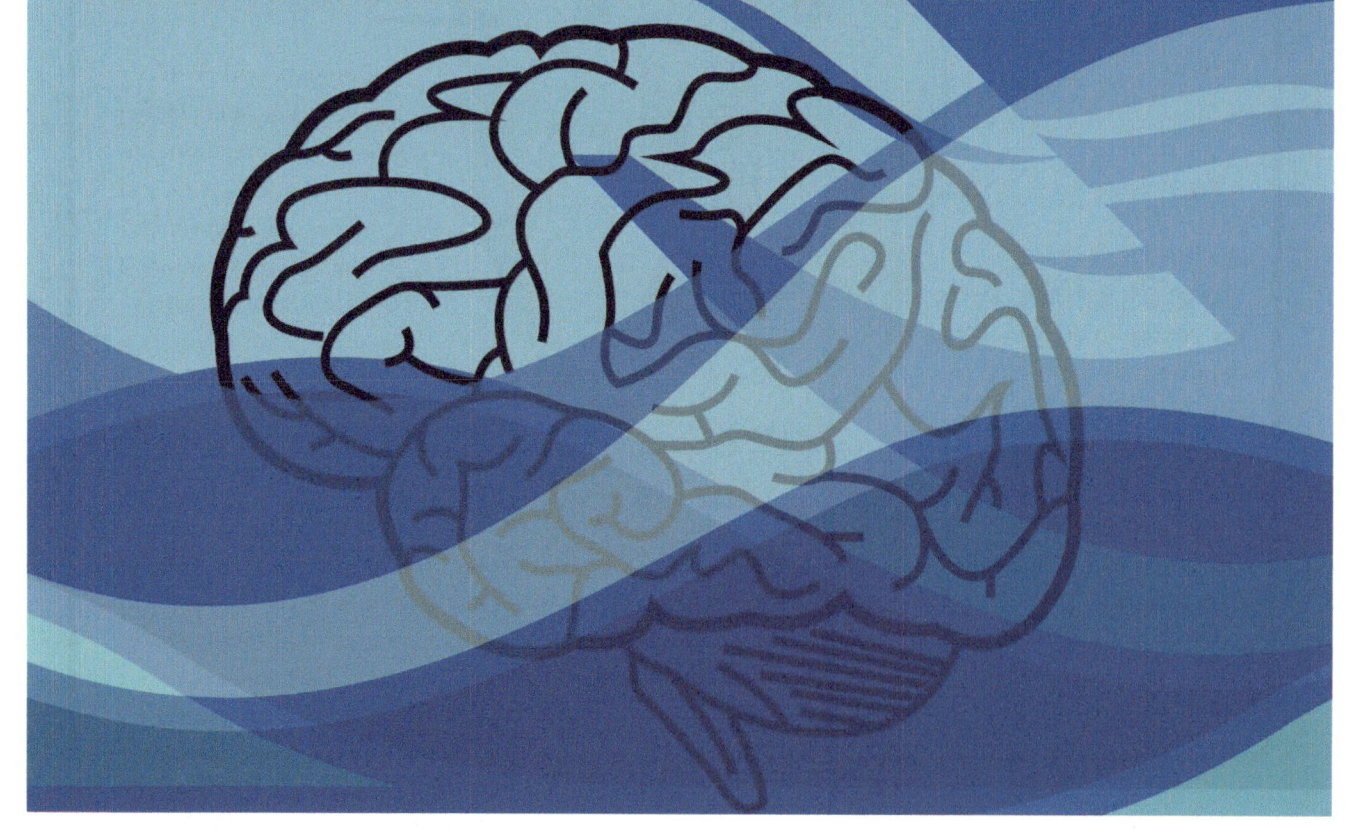

- Awareness: Our immediate awareness of our surroundings, thoughts, and emotions
- Control: Has a sense of control over our thoughts and actions
- Processing: Active and deliberate processing of information
- Capacity: Limited, as we can only focus on a limited amount of information at any given time
- Will: Closely linked to our sense of free will and known desires

History of Astrology

The study of astrology has a long and rich history, with roots dating back thousands of years to ancient civilizations like Egypt, Babylon, and Greece. These cultures used astrology to help them understand the patterns and movements of the stars and planets, which they believed held important information about the world and their place in it. Over time, astrology evolved into a more complex system, incorporating ideas from philosophy, mythology, and mathematics.

During the Renaissance, astrology experienced a resurgence in popularity and was considered a respected field of study. However, with the rise of science and skepticism in the 17th and 18th centuries, astrology faced criticism and eventually fell out of favor with the mainstream. With the introduction of new technology making it easier to access and understand, there has been a resurgence in using astrology to better understand our personal energy and that of the world. Consequently, many find value in astrology as a tool for self-discovery and personal growth.

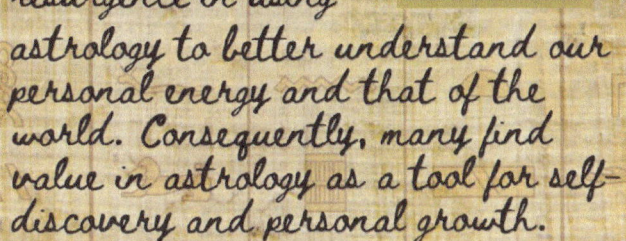

> "We are spiritual beings having a human experience."
> ~Pierre Teilhard de Chardin

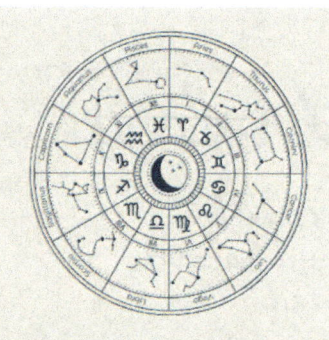

Natal Chart

What is required of you:

- Birth Date
- Birth Time
- Birth City

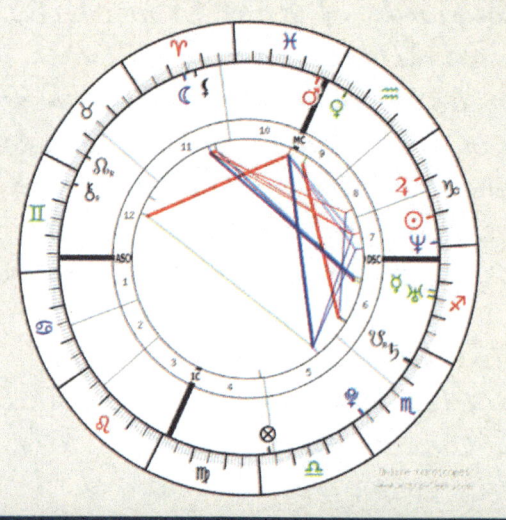

○ Sun
☽ Moon
☿ Mercury
♀ Venus
♂ Mars
♃ Jupiter
♄ Saturn
♅ Uranus
♆ Neptune
♇ Pluto

A natal chart is a map of the sky at the moment of your birth, showing the positions of the planets and other celestial bodies. Understanding your natal chart can provide insight into your energy, including strengths, weaknesses, and life purpose.

Step 1: Obtain your natal chart
There are many online websites that can generate your natal chart for free. Simply enter your birth date, time, and location to get an accurate chart.

Step 2: Identify the 12 houses
The natal chart is divided into 12 sections, called houses. Each house represents a different area of life, such as relationships, finances, career, and health.

Step 3: Identify the planets
The chart will show the positions of the sun, moon, and other planets at the time of your birth. Pay attention to the planets in your chart, the sign they are in, and their positions in the houses.

Step 4: Interpret the meaning of the planets
Each planet in astrology represents different qualities, such as love (Venus), communication (Mercury), and ambition (Mars). Look at where each planet is located in your chart, the sign, and what house it rules to understand its influence in your life.

Step 5: Study the aspects
The aspects in your natal chart show the relationships between the planets. Look at the angles between each planet and consider the meaning of the aspect. For example, a trine aspect is considered harmonious and supportive, while a square aspect is considered challenging.

Step 6: Look at your sun sign
Your sun sign is determined by the position of the sun in your chart at the time of your birth. This is the most well-known astrological sign and can provide insight into your basic energy.

Step 7: Reflect on what you've learned
Take some time to reflect on what you've learned from your natal chart. Consider what insights you've gained into yourself and your life path, and think about what steps you can take to nurture your strengths and work on your weaknesses.

PISCES SUN VIBES

Discover the Authentic You

Our authentic self is the truest expression of who we are as individuals, without the influence of external pressures or societal expectations. It is the part of ourselves that is most in tune with our deepest desires, values, and passions.

Living in alignment with our authentic self involves being true to ourselves, even if it means going against the norms or expectations of others. It involves embracing our unique strengths, talents, and quirks and expressing ourselves in a way that feels genuine and authentic.

When we are living in alignment with our authentic self, we experience a greater sense of fulfillment, meaning, and purpose in our lives. We feel more connected to ourselves and others, and we are able to tap into our innate creativity, intuition, and wisdom.

Exploring your natal chart can provide insight into your authentic self and help you better understand your natural energy. This guide is intended to help you with the process of discovering your authentic self.

Planet	Energy	Sign	House
Sun	how you express your core identity and individuality		
Moon	how you process and express your emotions.		
Rising	your outer personality, influencing first impressions, socializing		
Mercury	how you communicate and process information		
Venus	how you experience and express love, beauty, and pleasure		
Mars	how you assert yourself and pursue your goals		
Jupiter	where you seek growth and expansion in your life		
Saturn	where you experience limitations and challenges in your life		
Neptune	how you rebel against the norm and seek to express your unique self		
Uranus	where you experience creativity, spirituality, and inspiration		
Pluto	where you experience transformation, power, and change in your life		

When we don't live in alignment with our authentic selves, we experience a sense of disconnection, dissatisfaction, or even inner turmoil. Living out of alignment can manifest in a number of ways, including feeling unfulfilled in career or relationships, a sense of emptiness or lack of purpose, or constantly trying to fit in or meet the expectations of others, rather than expressing your true self.

Living inauthentically can also lead to physical and emotional symptoms, such as stress, anxiety, depression, or chronic health issues. When we are not living in alignment with our true selves, we may experience a sense of dis-ease or imbalance in our bodies and minds.

The good news is that it's never too late to realign with our authentic selves. By cultivating self-awareness, exploring our values and passions, and taking steps to express ourselves authentically, we can begin to live a more fulfilling, joyful, and purposeful life.

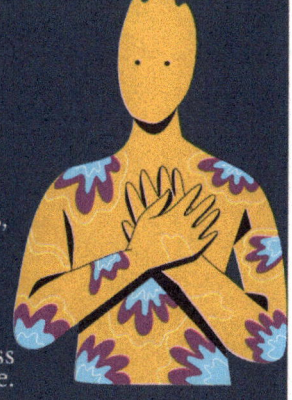

THE SUN

The Sun in astrology represents our core energy and our sense of self. Like the center of the solar system, it represents the center of your universe and the core of your identity. The sign the Sun is in (based on your birthday) reveals a lot about your natural energy: how you express yourself, what drives you, and what you want to be recognized for. Understanding and embracing your Sun sign energy can help you align with your authentic self and express yourself more confidently.

In a birth chart, the house that the Sun is in represents the area of life where you are most likely to express your sense of self and shine your brightest. You will spend your life growing into the highest expression of your Sun energy.

SUN = CONSCIOUS SELF

- Personal Power
- Ego
- Confidence
- Self-expression
- Creativity
- Best Self

The Pisces constellation gets its name from the Latin word for fish, as it is made up of stars that form the shape of two fish swimming in opposite directions. It is visible from both the Northern and Southern Hemispheres and one of the largest and most easily recognizable constellations in the night sky. It is located between the constellations of Aquarius and Aries and most visible during the months of October through January.

PISCES
CONSTELLATION

The Pisces constellation is home to many interesting stars and objects, including the famous M74 spiral galaxy, which is located approximately 30 million light years away from Earth. It also contains several notable stars, including Eta Piscium, a multiple star system visible to the naked eye, and Fomalhaut, one of the brightest stars in the night sky which is located on the southern edge of the constellation.

NEPTUNE

Neptune is known for its mysterious and ethereal qualities, and is often associated with creativity, spirituality, and the unseen or intangible realms. As the modern ruler of Pisces, Neptune amplifies the sign's sensitive, intuitive, and empathetic nature. Pisces individuals are said to be particularly attuned to the spiritual or mystical realms, and may have a deep connection to the collective unconscious or the hidden aspects of human experience.

Neptune is also associated with illusions, deception, and confusion, and Pisces individuals may be prone to escapism or a tendency to avoid confrontation or unpleasant truths.

Jupiter, the planet of expansion and growth, is the traditional ruler of Pisces. This brings an inherent optimism, wisdom, and desire for spiritual and emotional growth to the Pisces energy, fostering their imagination, compassion, and deep intuitive sense.

The ruling planet of a zodiac sign is considered to be the planet that has the most influence over that sign's energy profile, because the ruling planet is believed to represent the energies and qualities that are most closely aligned with the sign's nature. Knowledge of the ruling planet can provide insight into the core energy and areas of growth of a sign. Understanding the ruling planet can provide guidance for working with the energies of a sign in a positive and productive way and can be used to enhance personal growth and self-awareness.

Water signs focus on emotional energy. Cancer is to create nurturing environments, by fostering emotional connections and offering support and care to others. Scorpio is to undergo transformative experiences, by exploring the depths of emotions and using their intensity to heal and empower themselves and others. Pisces is to tap into spiritual realms, by channeling empathy and creativity and using their compassionate nature to bring healing and unity to the world.

WATER SIGN ENERGY

CANCER   SCORPIO   PISCES

Emotional Intelligence: Water signs are in touch with their emotions, allowing them to easily understand and empathize with others.

Compassionate: They are nurturing and often put others' needs before their own.

Creative: Water signs are imaginative and creative, often finding unique and artistic solutions to problems.

Intuitive: They trust their gut instincts and are often able to see the hidden meaning in things.

Overly Emotional: Water signs can become overwhelmed by their emotions and may struggle to manage their feelings.

Sensitive: They are highly sensitive to criticism and rejection, and can take things very personally.

Indecisive: Water signs may struggle with making decisions, as they often consider all the possible outcomes and feel torn in different directions.

Reactive: They may react strongly to emotional triggers and have trouble regulating their emotions.

Pisces' journey involves finding balance between their idealistic nature and the need for self-care and boundaries.

RELEASE THE STEAM

- Practice self-care and find healthy ways to manage your emotions.
- Develop healthy boundaries to protect your emotional well-being.
- Work on making decisions by weighing options and taking action, even if it's not perfect.
- Learn techniques for regulating your emotions, such as mindfulness or deep breathing.

PISCES SUN VIBES

Pisces Sun expresses mutable energy through their emotional awareness. Their goal is to expand and reshape emotional energy by adapting their dreams and reality based on their intuition and spirituality.

Flexibility: Mutable signs are known for their adaptability and ability to change. They can easily shift gears and adjust to new situations.

Versatility: Mutable signs are often multi-talented and can do a little bit of everything.

Communication skills: Mutable signs, especially Gemini, have strong verbal skills.

Open-mindedness: Mutable signs are often accepting of different perspectives and enjoy exploring new ideas.

GEMINI

VIRGO

SAGITTARIUS

PISCES

FLEXIBLE

MUTABLE
SIGN ENERGY

Mutable energy demonstrates its adaptive nature by adjusting to the surrounding environment and expressing its elemental qualities in a modified and flexible manner.

MUTABLE SIGN ENERGY

Indecisive: Mutable signs can struggle with making decisions because they see the value in many options.
Restless: They may have difficulty sticking to one thing for an extended period of time.
Difficulty with commitment: Mutable signs can be hesitant to commit to one path or relationship, due to their desire for flexibility.
Lack of boundaries: They may struggle to set boundaries, as they often have a tendency to over-extend themselves.

GEMINI VIRGO SAGITTARIUS PISCES

PISCES SUN VIBES

EMOTIONALLY TUNED IN

Energy is a fundamental force that is responsible for creating and sustaining movement, activity, and life. In the context of emotions, thoughts, and behaviors, energy can be thought of as a vibrational frequency. Different emotions, thoughts, and behaviors can be associated with different frequencies of energy.

High vibrational energy is associated with positive emotions, thoughts, and behaviors. People with high vibrational energy tend to be optimistic, compassionate, and empathetic. They are open to new experiences, and approach life with a sense of curiosity and wonder. High vibrational energy can have a positive impact on an individual's life. It can help them to attract positive experiences and opportunities, cultivate better relationships, and promote greater well-being. People with high vibrational energy tend to be happier, more fulfilled, and more successful in life.

HIGH FREQUENCY

Love   Joy   Gratitude
Forgiveness   Compassion   Empathy
Open-mindedness   Creativity
Inspiration   Curiosity

LOW FREQUENCY

Fear   Anger   Resentment   Jealousy
Envy   Cynicism   Skepticism   Pessimism
Judgmental   Closed-mindedness

Low vibrational energy, on the other hand, is associated with negative emotions, thoughts, and behaviors. People with low vibrational energy tend to be pessimistic, judgmental, and closed-minded. They may be resistant to change and approach life with a sense of cynicism and skepticism. Low vibrational energy can limit an individual's potential and lead to negative outcomes. It can contribute to feelings of stress, anxiety, and depression, and may lead to strained relationships and missed opportunities.

Everyone has good days and bad days. Remember, raising your vibration does not mean ignoring or suppressing your emotions but rather acknowledging and processing them in a healthy way. By processing and releasing negative emotions, you create space for positive emotions and higher frequencies to flow into your life.

HOW TO RAISE YOUR VIBRATION

What emotions do you experience most frequently?

1 Gratitude journaling: Each day, write down three things you are grateful for. This can help shift your focus towards the positive things in your life and promote feelings of joy and contentment.

What thoughts or behaviors do you engage in that may be limiting your potential?

2 Meditation: Spend 10-15 minutes each day in meditation, focusing on your breath and letting go of negative thoughts and emotions. This can help you feel more calm and centered, and promote greater well-being.

3 Acts of kindness: Engage in acts of kindness towards others, such as helping a neighbor with groceries or sending a thoughtful message to a friend. This can help promote feelings of compassion and empathy, and contribute to a more positive outlook on life.

What are some areas of your life where you feel stuck or stagnant, and how can you shift your energy towards a more positive direction?

How can you cultivate more positive emotions, thoughts, and behaviors in your daily life?

4 Affirmations: Repeat positive affirmations to yourself throughout the day, such as "I am worthy of love and happiness" or "I trust in the universe to guide me towards my highest good". This can help shift your mindset towards a more positive and optimistic outlook.

PISCES SUN VIBES

When we operate from a higher expression of our natural energy, we are more likely to experience positive thoughts, emotions, and behaviors.

Pisces sun energy

CREATIVE
Pisces are original and inventive.

EMPATHETIC
Pisces are compassionate and sensitive.

INTUITIVE
Pisces are perceptive and instinctive.

GENEROUS
Pisces are giving and altruistic.

ADAPTABLE
Pisces are faithful and devoted.

Sun energy represents our core identity, what we stand for, and what we aim to achieve in life. When your sun energy is positive, you embody qualities that help you manifest your goals and desires. This energy is in alignment with your authentic self and brings you joy and fulfillment.

Pisces

Pisces Energy
CREATIVE

- Comes up with new ideas and unique solutions
- Enjoys arts and crafts

Pisces suns are known for their vivid imagination and creativity. They often have a unique and artistic perspective that allows them to see the world in a different way.

A wise man never knows all, only fools know everything.
~African Proverb

How can you incorporate more creativity into your daily life?

PISCES SUN VIBES

Creativity Generator

What if...? Imagine a different reality or scenario

Create a collage

Brainstorm different ideas for creative projects or endeavors that stem from each question or inspiration.

How might we...? Come up with potential solutions to a problem or challenge

What if we tried...? Consider new or unconventional ideas for a project

What are the possibilities...? Think expansively

Write a short story

Create a poem or song

Create a visual mood board

Experiment with abstract art

What are the potential obstacles...? Consider potential roadblocks or challenges

How can we improve...? Enhance or optimize an existing process or system

Pisces

Pisces Energy
EMPATHETIC

- Offers a shoulder to cry on
- Helps to solve others' problems

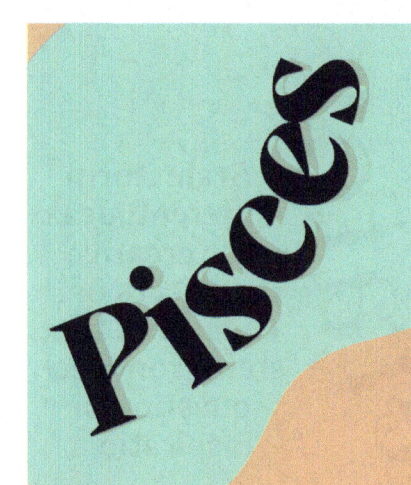

Pisces are very empathetic and compassionate, and are known for their ability to understand and connect with others on an emotional level.

The one who loves an unsightly person is the one who makes him beautiful.
—African Proverb

How can you practice self-compassion and understanding towards yourself?

PISCES SUN VIBES

Empathy in Action

WRITE THE WAYS THAT YOU CAN SHOW EMPATHY AND SUPPORT TO THE PEOPLE IN EACH SCENARIO.

Whitley has just lost her job, and she's struggling to make ends meet. She's worried about how she's going to pay her bills and support her family, and she feels like a failure for not being able to provide for them.

Adam has recently gone through a painful breakup, and he's having a hard time moving on. He finds himself constantly thinking about his ex-partner and replaying old memories in his head, which leaves him feeling sad and lonely.

Marie has been dealing with chronic pain for several years, and it's starting to take a toll on her mental health. She's tired of feeling like she's always in pain, and she's frustrated that no one seems to understand what she's going through.

Tyrese has just received a cancer diagnosis, and he's struggling to come to terms with the news. He's scared about what the future holds, and he's worried about the impact that his illness will have on his loved ones.

Lakeisha is going through a difficult divorce, and she's struggling to cope with the emotional fallout. She feels betrayed and hurt by her ex-partner, and she's worried about how the divorce will impact their children.

Michael has been dealing with anxiety and depression for several years, and it's become increasingly difficult for him to manage his symptoms. He feels like he's constantly on edge and can't enjoy life the way he used to, which leaves him feeling hopeless and isolated.

SELF love

THE CHOICE TO ACCEPT, APPRECIATE, PROTECT AND BE GENTLE WITH YOURSELF.

- BE PROUD OF YOUR ACHIEVEMENTS
- FORGIVE YOURSELF
- SET HEALTHY BOUNDARIES
- ACCEPT HELP
- KNOW AND ACCEPT YOUR FEELINGS
- LISTEN TO YOUR BODY
- SAY NO TO COMPARISONS AND SELF JUDGEMENT
- TRUST YOURSELF
- THINK, SPEAK AND TALK TO YOURSELF WITH KINDNESS

Learning to set boundaries can help you avoid overextending yourself and maintain healthier relationships with others and yourself.

Emotions Check In

You can't manage your emotions if you don't know how you are feeling! A periodic emotions check-in helps you to identify your emotions and their intensity.

START

How are you feeling out of 10?

/10

Describe how you're feeling in 3 words.

If you need to, do you feel like you have someone trusted to talk to about how you feel?

☐ Yes
☐ No

if yes...

Who can you talk to?
☐ Parent/guardian
☐ Sibling
☐ Other family member
☐ Teacher
☐ Friend
☐ Counselor
☐ Someone else

if no...

Call 911 if you or someone you know is in immediate danger or go to the nearest emergency room

not an emergency

FINISH

Text "HELLO" to 741741 The Crisis Text hotline serves anyone, in any type of crisis, connecting them with a crisis counselor who can provide support and information.

My emotions are a source of my strength. I honor them, learn from them, and allow them to deepen my understanding of myself and the world around me.

PISCES SUN VIBES

Pisces

Pisces Energy
INTUITIVE

Recognize things below the surface

Picks up on subtle energy shifts

Pisces possess exceptional intuition, which enables them to make well-informed decisions and skillfully navigate life's challenges.

The journey is more important than the destination.
~African Proverb

How has my intuition guided me in the past, and how can I continue to develop this skill?

SHONETTE CHARLES

Is it Intuition?

Reading a good book can be a great way to relax and escape from the stresses of everyday life.

Intuition is our inner voice or gut feeling that helps us make decisions and guide us in our daily lives. It is a unique sense that allows us to understand things without necessarily knowing how or why.

Common Ways Your Intuition Communicates

A gut feeling or inner knowing that something is right or wrong

Physical sensations such as tingling, tightness, or discomfort in your body

A sense of peace or calm when thinking about a particular decision or action

Synchronicities or meaningful coincidences that seem to guide you in a particular direction

Dreams or vivid imagery that provide insight or guidance

Emotional responses such as fear, excitement, or curiosity

A sudden shift in mood or perspective that feels like an "aha" moment

An inner voice or dialogue that offers guidance or advice

Unexplained flashes of insight or inspiration

A sense of clarity or certainty that comes from within

These signs and signals may manifest differently for different people, and may also change over time or in different situations. The key is to stay attuned to your inner experience and trust the signals that feel authentic and aligned with your true self.

You are walking home at night and feel a sense of unease as you pass a dark alley. You decide to cross the street and continue on your way. Is this an example of intuition or rational thinking?

You are trying to decide whether to take a job that offers a high salary but requires long hours and a long commute, or a job that offers a lower salary but allows for more work-life balance. You make a list of the pros and cons of each option and weigh them carefully. Is this an example of intuition or rational thinking?

You are in a conversation with a friend who has been struggling with depression, and you suddenly get a strong sense that you should invite them to a support group that you recently heard about. Is this an example of intuition or rational thinking?

You are planning a vacation and are trying to decide between two destinations. One is a popular tourist spot with lots of amenities, and the other is a remote wilderness area with beautiful scenery. You consult with travel guides and online reviews to gather more information. Is this an example of intuition or rational thinking?

You are considering starting a new business venture but are feeling anxious and unsure about the risks involved. You take some time to meditate and journal about your feelings and notice a sense of clarity and excitement about the project. Is this an example of intuition or rational thinking?

PISCES SUN VIBES

DREAM JOURNAL

When you wake up in the morning, write down everything you remember about your dreams, including the setting, characters, emotions, and events. Don't worry about writing in complete sentences or making sense of the dream right away; just focus on capturing as much detail as possible.

- What was the setting of your dream?
- Who was in your dream?
- What emotions did you feel during the dream?
- What events or actions took place in the dream?
- What symbols or images appeared in the dream?

Look for recurring symbols or themes in your dreams. Do you often dream about water, flying, or being chased? Do certain people or animals show up frequently in your dreams? Pay attention to these patterns and see if you can find any meaning or symbolism in them.

You owe yourself to become everything you've ever dreamed of being.

Reflect on the emotions and feelings that come up in your dreams. Do you feel happy, scared, anxious, or excited in your dreams? Are there any unresolved issues or conflicts that are coming up in your dreams? Use your dream journal as a space to explore these feelings and gain insight into your inner world.

Consider how your dreams relate to your waking life. Are there any connections between your dreams and your thoughts, feelings, or experiences during the day? Use your dream journal to reflect on these connections and see how your dreams can offer guidance, inspiration, or insight into your waking life.

25

Dream Journal

WHAT HAPPENED?

MY EMOTIONS

RECURRING?

MY INTERPRETATION

Pisces

Pisces Energy
GENEROUS

Helps others when they are in need

Considerate and Protecting

Pisces suns are often described as selfless and giving, and are known for their willingness to help others and make sacrifices for the people they love.

When spider webs unite, they can tie up a lion.
~African Proverb

Role Play Scenario: Act out a scenario where you offer a kind word or gesture to someone in need and brighten their day.

GIVING PLAN

Learn to treat yourself with kindness and understanding to build greater self-confidence and resilience.

Take some time to reflect on the many ways that you give to others and list them below.

Time

Skills

Resources

Voice

Are there any areas where you would like to give more?

Are there any areas where you would like to give less?

Think about the impact you hope to have through your giving. How do you want to make a difference in the lives of others? What outcomes do you hope to achieve?

With an open heart, I generously give to others while maintaining healthy boundaries that protect and nurture my own well-being.

FILL EACH DAY WITH *Gratitude*

3 SMALL THINGS I APPRECIATE TODAY

3 GOOD THINGS THAT HAPPENED TODAY

TODAY'S POSITIVE AFFIRMATION

MY FAVORITE MOMENTS OF THE DAY

Gratitude is a powerful tool for fostering optimism and a positive outlook on life. When we focus on the things that we are thankful for, it helps to shift our attention away from what is wrong or what we lack. It also helps us to see all the good that is in our lives. This can lead to an overall increase in happiness, hope, and positivity.

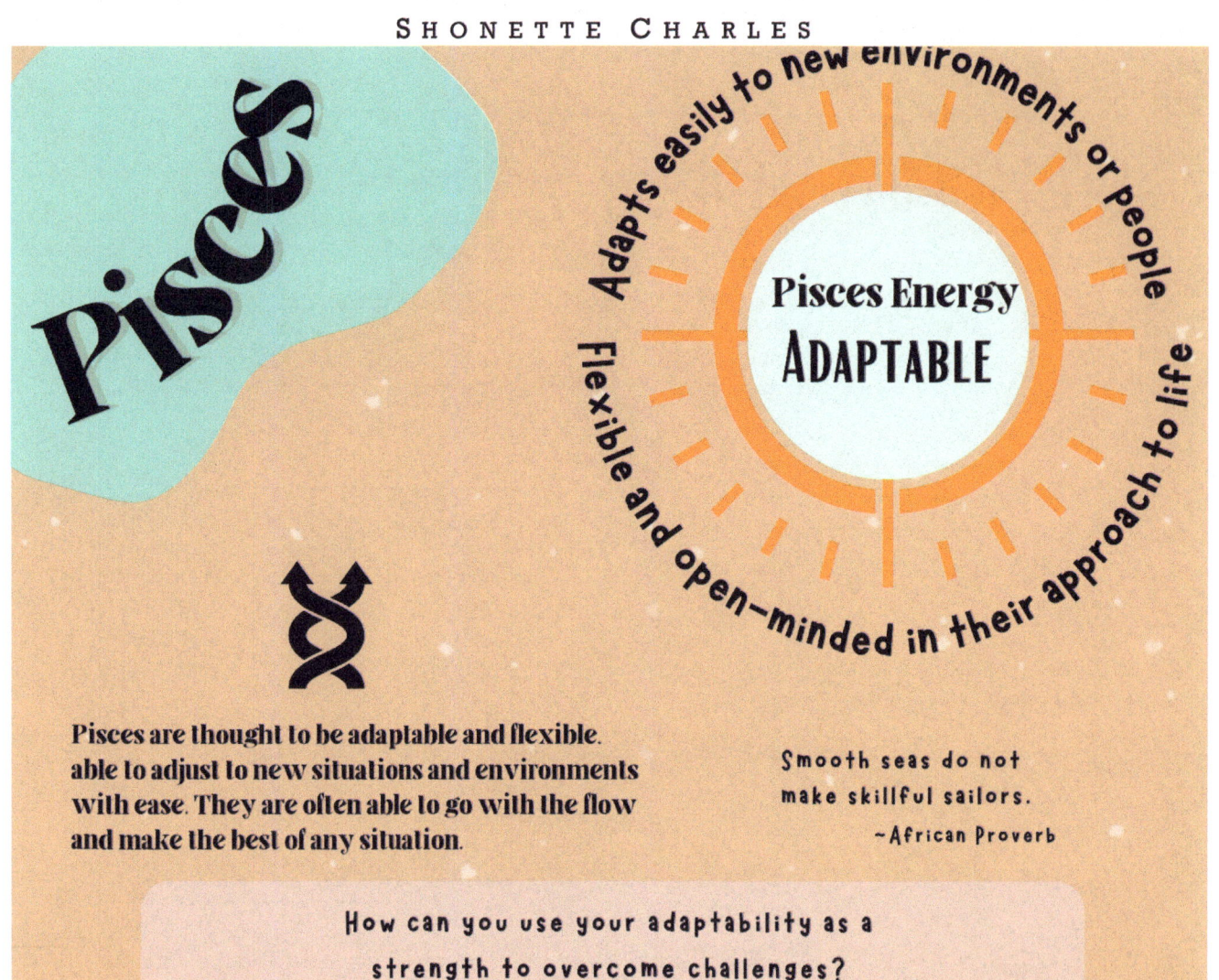

Pisces

Pisces Energy
ADAPTABLE

Adapts easily to new environments or people

Flexible and open-minded in their approach to life

Pisces are thought to be adaptable and flexible, able to adjust to new situations and environments with ease. They are often able to go with the flow and make the best of any situation.

> Smooth seas do not make skillful sailors.
> ~African Proverb

How can you use your adaptability as a strength to overcome challenges?

PISCES SUN VIBES

PISCES RESILIENCE *shield*

Pisces suns are adaptable and able to withstand setbacks. Write words or draw pictures to represent what strengthens your resilience shield.

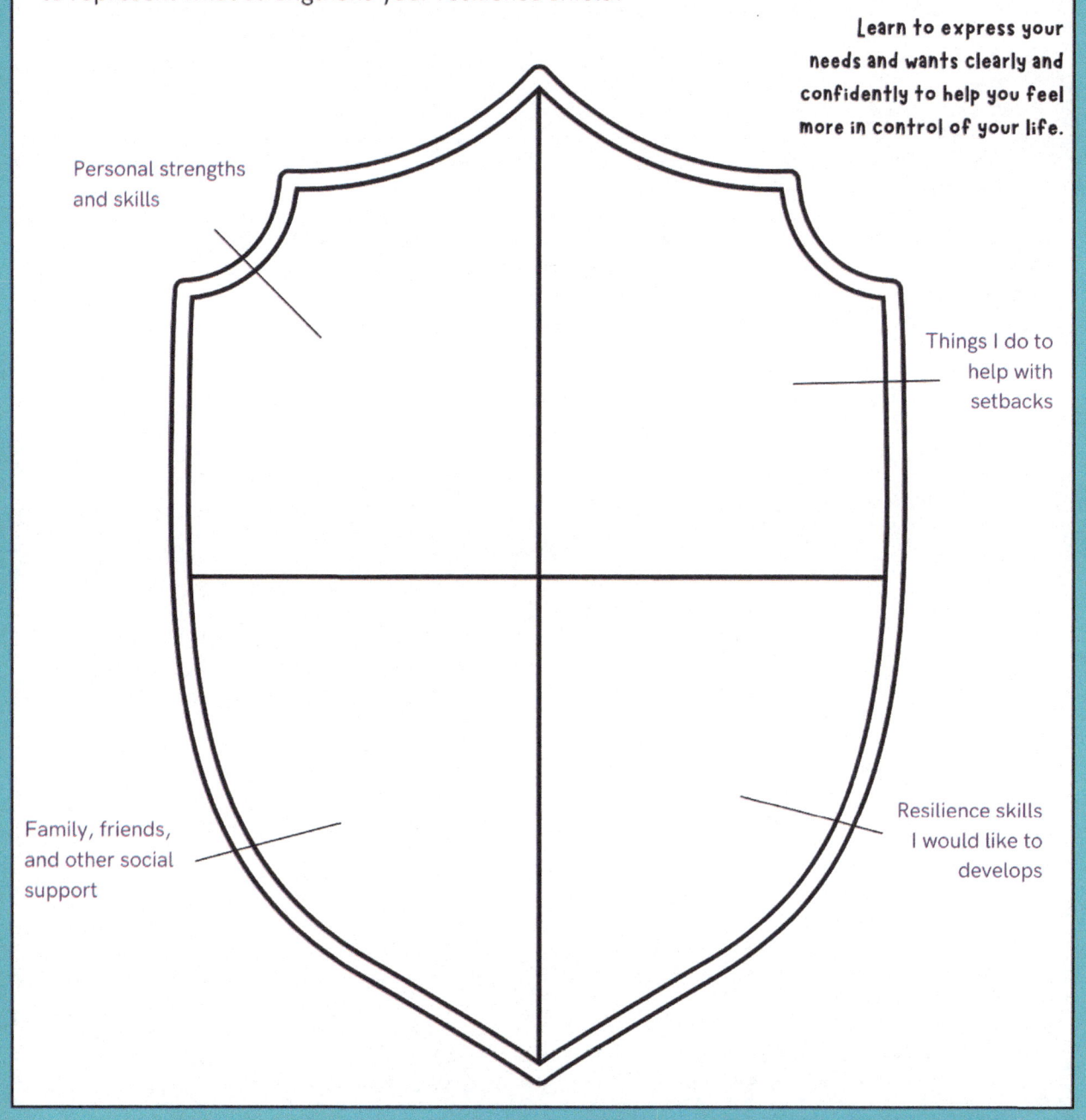

Learn to express your needs and wants clearly and confidently to help you feel more in control of your life.

- Personal strengths and skills
- Things I do to help with setbacks
- Family, friends, and other social support
- Resilience skills I would like to develops

What does "equal energy exchange" mean to you?

Write a brief definition and what it looks like in a friendship.

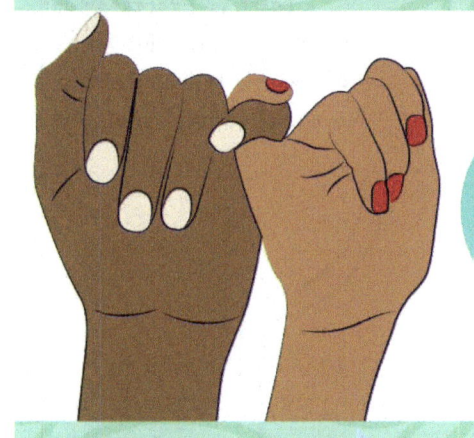

EQUAL ENERGY
EXCHANGE

Think about one of your current friendships. Does the energy exchange feel equal?

In what ways do you give energy to this friendship? Examples might include spending time together, offering support, or sharing personal information.

Explain what makes you feel this way, and if not, what you would like to see change.

In what ways does your friend give energy back to you? Examples might include spending time together, offering support, or sharing personal information.

Do you feel like the energy exchange is balanced? Why or why not?

Remember that equal energy exchange does not always mean that both friends give and receive energy in exactly the same ways. It means that both friends feel like they are getting what they need from the friendship. By reflecting on this concept and taking steps to balance energy exchange, you can build stronger, healthier friendships.

What steps can you take to create a more balanced energy exchange in this friendship?

Repeat steps 2-6 for other friendships.

How will you use what you've learned to strengthen your current and future friendships?

GROWING UP A PISCES SUN

1. Preschool
2. Elementary
3. Tween
4. Teenager
5. Adult

I am a vessel of compassion, navigating the currents of life with empathy and understanding.

Pisces' evolution lies in transcending the boundaries of the material world, surrendering to the flow of life, and channeling their empathy and creativity into compassionate service.

PISCES SUN VIBES

1

Pisces Sun preschoolers may have a vivid imagination, sensitivity to others' emotions, and a desire for comfort and security. Children with Pisces Sun may have a rich inner world and find comfort in imaginative play and creative expression, such as art or music. They could also be prone to mood swings or emotional outbursts and may need extra support and reassurance during times of stress or change.

2

Pisces Sun children have a growing interest in spirituality, creativity, and empathy. Children with Pisces Sun may have a deep sensitivity to others' emotions and be drawn to helping those in need. They could also have a vivid imagination and find fulfillment in artistic or imaginative pursuits. However, they may struggle with practical matters such as organization or discipline and need extra support and guidance to develop these skills.

3

Pisces Sun tweens may be drawn to spiritual or metaphysical pursuits and be interested in exploring their inner world through meditation or introspection. They could also have a strong desire to help others and find fulfillment in creative or artistic expression. However, they may struggle with self-doubt or confusion and need extra support and validation to build their self-esteem.

4

Pisces Sun teens may be drawn to artistic or mystical pursuits and find fulfillment in expressing themselves through music, writing, or other forms of creative expression. They could also have a deep empathy for others and be drawn to social justice or service work. However, they may struggle with self-doubt or uncertainty about their place in the world and need extra support and guidance to build their self-confidence and develop a sense of purpose.

5

Pisces Sun adults may be drawn to healing or service professions and find fulfillment in using their gifts to uplift others. They may also have a strong connection to the spiritual or mystical realms and be drawn to metaphysical or esoteric pursuits. However, they may struggle with boundaries and need to cultivate greater self-awareness and emotional honesty to maintain healthy relationships and achieve their goals.

When we operate from a lower expression of our natural energy, we are more likely to experience negative thoughts, emotions, and behaviors. Low vibrational energies can create a sense of discord or disconnection from oneself and the world around us, leading to a sense of dissatisfaction or unhappiness.

Pisces shadow energy

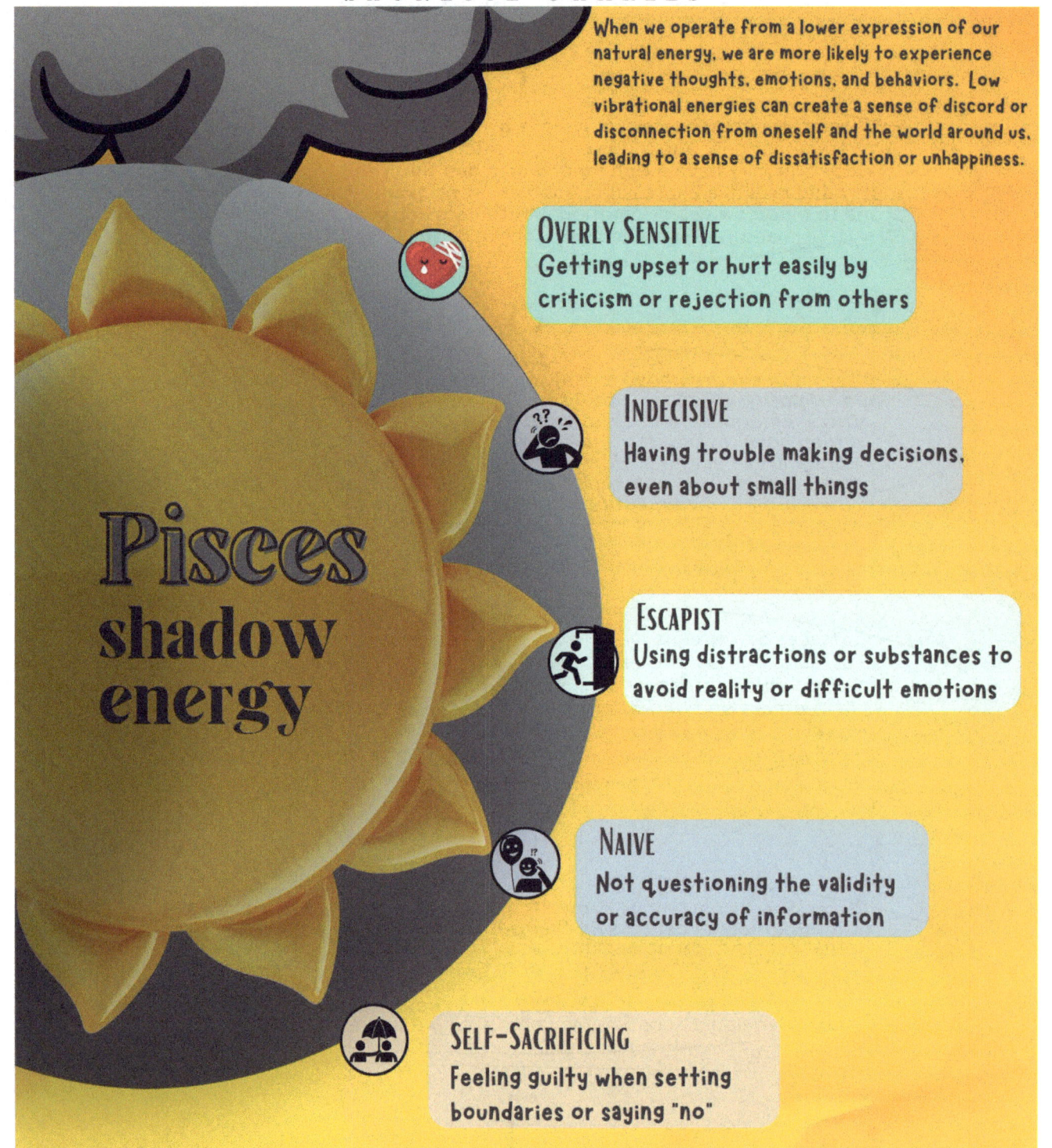

OVERLY SENSITIVE
Getting upset or hurt easily by criticism or rejection from others

INDECISIVE
Having trouble making decisions, even about small things

ESCAPIST
Using distractions or substances to avoid reality or difficult emotions

NAIVE
Not questioning the validity or accuracy of information

SELF-SACRIFICING
Feeling guilty when setting boundaries or saying "no"

When sun energy is in shadow, it manifests negative energy. This shadow energy often stems from unresolved issues or insecurities. Recognizing and accepting the shadow of one's sun energy can help to integrate these aspects. Using tools and methods at your disposal will allow you to transform this negative energy into positive, thereby enhancing overall well-being.

PISCES SUN VIBES

Pisces

Shadow Energy: OVERLY SENSITIVE

In their shadow, Pisces are very sensitive, which can sometimes cause them to be overly emotional or take things too personally.

Practice: POSITIVE AFFIRMATIONS

What situations or experiences trigger your sensitivity? How can you respond in a way that honors your emotions while still setting healthy boundaries?

SENSITIVITY

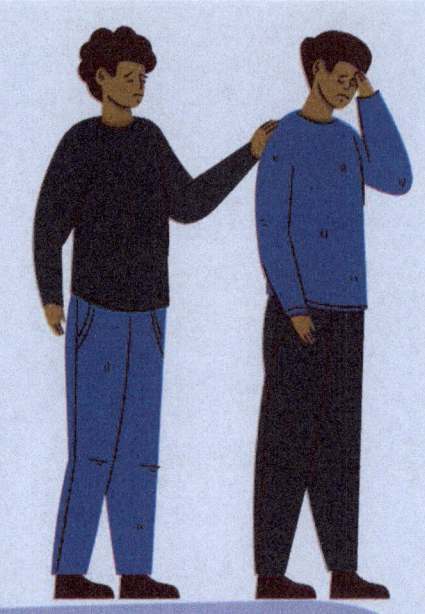

Common triggers that cause people to become overly emotional or sensitive:

- Criticism or negative feedback
- Conflict with others
- Overwhelm from work or responsibilities
- Lack of control over a situation
- Feeling invalidated or dismissed by others
- Trauma or past emotional experiences

What triggers your sensitivity the most? Are there any patterns or themes that you notice in these triggers?

What are some coping strategies that you use in these situations? What are others that you could develop?

TRIGGERS

Physical and emotional sensations that people experience when they are triggered:

Increased heart rate and breathing
Sweating or shaking
Tightness in the chest or throat
Feeling hot or flushed
Racing thoughts or feelings of panic
Intense emotional reactions

PISCES SUN VIBES

When was the last time you felt hurt or upset by something someone said or did? How did you react in the moment, and how did you feel afterward?

Do you feel like you're often on high alert for criticism or negativity from others? Why do you think this might be the case?

Containing Over-Sensitivity

What are some situations or types of interactions that tend to trigger your sensitivity? Why do you think this might be the case?

Are there certain people or relationships in your life that tend to bring out your sensitivity more than others? What might be contributing to this dynamic?

BODY SCAN MEDITATION

Pisces suns are often drawn to bodies of water, so spending time near the ocean, a lake, or a river can be very calming and rejuvenating for you.

Body Scan Meditation: Begin by finding a quiet, comfortable place to lie down. Close your eyes and take a few deep breaths, focusing on the sensation of the air moving in and out of your body. Then, starting at the top of your head, begin to scan down through your body, paying attention to any areas of tension or discomfort. As you move through each part of your body, breathe into the area and imagine releasing any tension or negativity. This can help you to become more aware of your physical sensations and connect with your inner wisdom.

LIST ANY CHANGES TO THE ENVIRONMENT

MARK WHERE YOU FELT SENSATIONS

FRONT　　BACK

WHAT MESSAGES OR INSIGHTS DID YOU RECEIVE?

HOW DO YOU FEEL ABOUT TUNING INTO YOUR BODY AND INTUITION IN THIS WAY?

PISCES SUN VIBES

Pisces

Shadow Energy: INDECISIVE

In their shadow, Pisces are thought to have a hard time making decisions, as they like to weigh all the options and can sometimes get lost in their own thoughts.

Practice: Weighing Pros and Cons

What are some factors that contribute to your indecisiveness? How can you work to overcome them?

SHONETTE CHARLES

MY VALUES

Being confident in decision-making involves recognizing when your choices align with your core values. By understanding your beliefs and goals, you can navigate life with clarity and make well-informed decisions that stay true to who you are.

LOVE

PURPOSE

SELF CARE

CREATIVITY

COMMUNITY

FRIENDSHIP

Write a value you hold in the box related to each category, then, give one example of how your actions are aligned with that value.

PISCES SUN VIBES

Pisces

Shadow Energy: ESCAPIST

In their shadow, Pisces are often described as escapist, as they may have a tendency to avoid reality and seek refuge in their imagination or through various forms of escapism.

Practice: PROBLEM SOLVING

Reflect on a recent situation where you found yourself wanting to escape or avoid dealing with a problem. What emotions or fears might have been driving this response? How could you approach such situations differently to face challenges head-on, rather than resorting to escapism?

SHONETTE CHARLES

RELAX, RELATE, RELEASE

IDENTIFY THE FEELING

Take a moment to identify what you're feeling. Label the emotion as best as you can (e.g. happy, sad, angry, frustrated).

ACKNOWLEDGE THE FEELING

Accept the feeling and allow yourself to experience it. Don't judge yourself for having the emotion.

EXPLORE THE FEELING

Try to understand why you're feeling the way you are. What triggered the emotion? What are the underlying thoughts and beliefs that are contributing to the feeling?

PRACTICE SELF-CARE

Engage in activities that make you feel good and calm. This can include exercise, meditation, talking to a friend, or engaging in a hobby.

REFRAME THE SITUATION

Try to look at the situation from a different perspective. What are the positive aspects of the situation? How can you shift your thinking to be more positive and proactive?

What are some activities or behaviors you engage in to escape difficult emotions or reality? How do you feel before, during, and after engaging in these activities?

What would happen if you stopped using escapism as a coping mechanism? How would your life be different?

What strategies or practices do you employ to understand and express your feelings? How do you create a safe and supportive space for yourself to process and heal?

PISCES SUN VIBES

Diving into Your Goals

Breaking down a big goal into smaller tasks can make it feel less overwhelming and more achievable.

1 Write down your goal.

2 Brainstorm smaller tasks that will need to happen to achieve your goal. Try to break the goal down into as many small tasks as you can.

3 Put the tasks in the correct order you will need to complete them. This will help you see the logical order of the tasks.

4 Set a deadline for each task. This will help you stay on track and make progress towards your goal.

5 Track your progress As you complete each task, check it off on the worksheet. This will help you see your progress and stay motivated.

PLOT YOUR GOALS

Goal:

Date: | Priority Tasks:

Notes: | Reminder:

45

DIVING INTO MY GOALS

Goal:

☑ **Date:** **Priority Tasks:**

☐

☐

☐

☐

☐

☐

☐

☐

Pisces can benefit from spending time in nature, which can help them connect with their inner selves and find a sense of peace and grounding.

Notes: **Reminders:**

PISCES SUN VIBES

Pisces

Shadow Energy: NAIVE

In their shadow, Pisces are thought to be trusting and may sometimes be too gullible or easily taken advantage of by others.

Practice: CRITICAL THINKING

What are some factors that make you susceptible to being taken advantage of, and how can you become more discerning and wise in your interactions with others?

Critical Thinking
DECISION TREE

The goal of the Critical Thinking Decision Tree is to help you make effective and thoughtful decisions by considering a range of factors and potential outcomes.

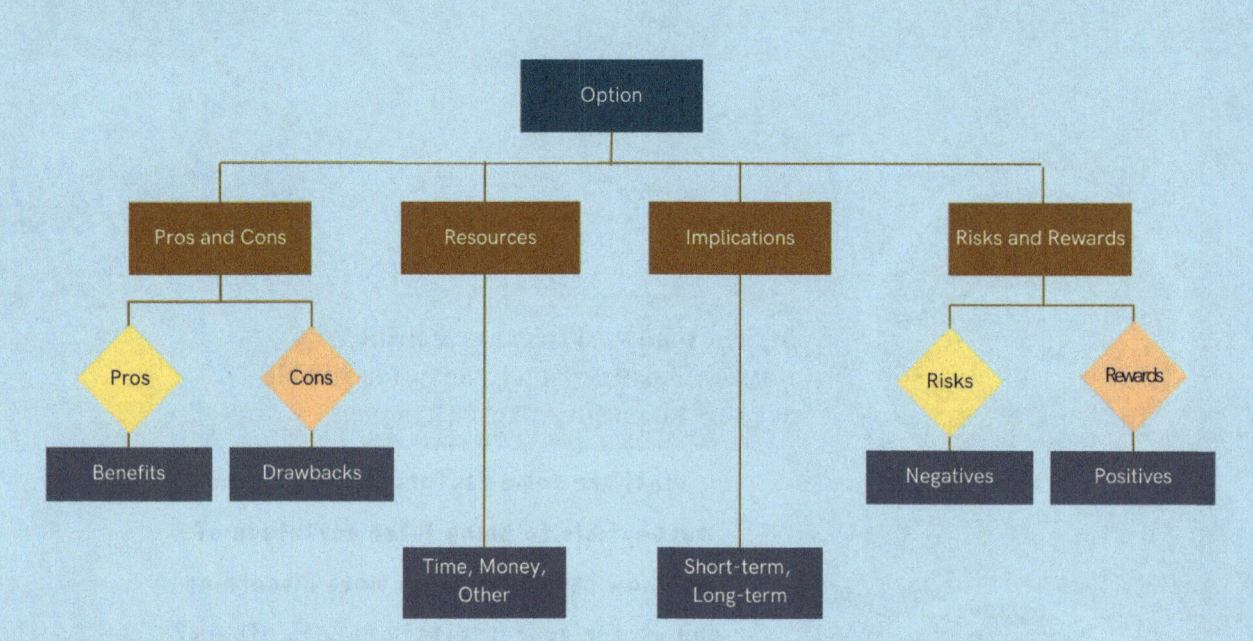

```
Option
├── Pros and Cons
│   ├── Pros → Benefits
│   └── Cons → Drawbacks
├── Resources → Time, Money, Other
├── Implications → Short-term, Long-term
└── Risks and Rewards
    ├── Risks → Negatives
    └── Rewards → Positives
```

How to Use:
Start by identifying the decision you need to make and the desired outcome or goal. Consider the potential options or courses of action available to you, and write them down. Use the answers to these questions to weigh the options against each other, and determine which one is most likely to lead to the desired outcome.

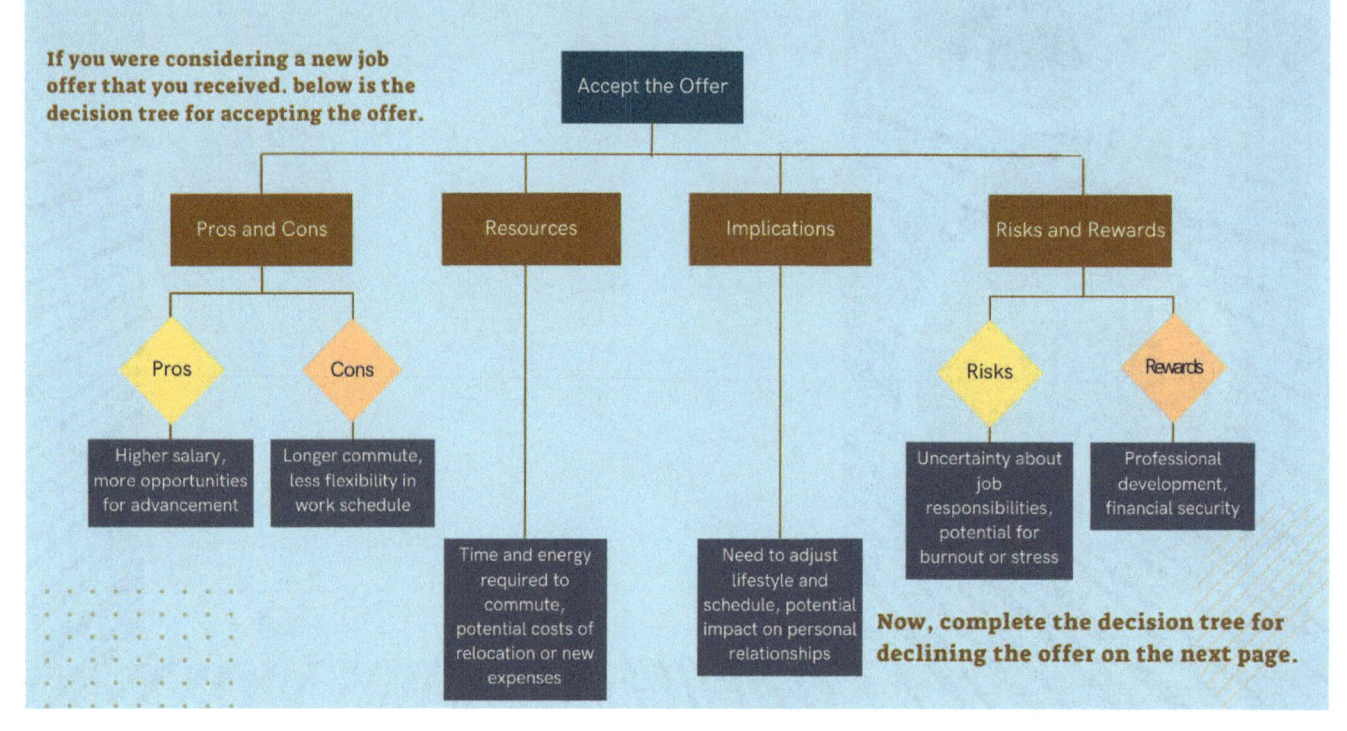

If you were considering a new job offer that you received, below is the decision tree for accepting the offer.

```
Accept the Offer
├── Pros and Cons
│   ├── Pros → Higher salary, more opportunities for advancement
│   └── Cons → Longer commute, less flexibility in work schedule
├── Resources → Time and energy required to commute, potential costs of relocation or new expenses
├── Implications → Need to adjust lifestyle and schedule, potential impact on personal relationships
└── Risks and Rewards
    ├── Risks → Uncertainty about job responsibilities, potential for burnout or stress
    └── Rewards → Professional development, financial security
```

Now, complete the decision tree for declining the offer on the next page.

PISCES SUN VIBES

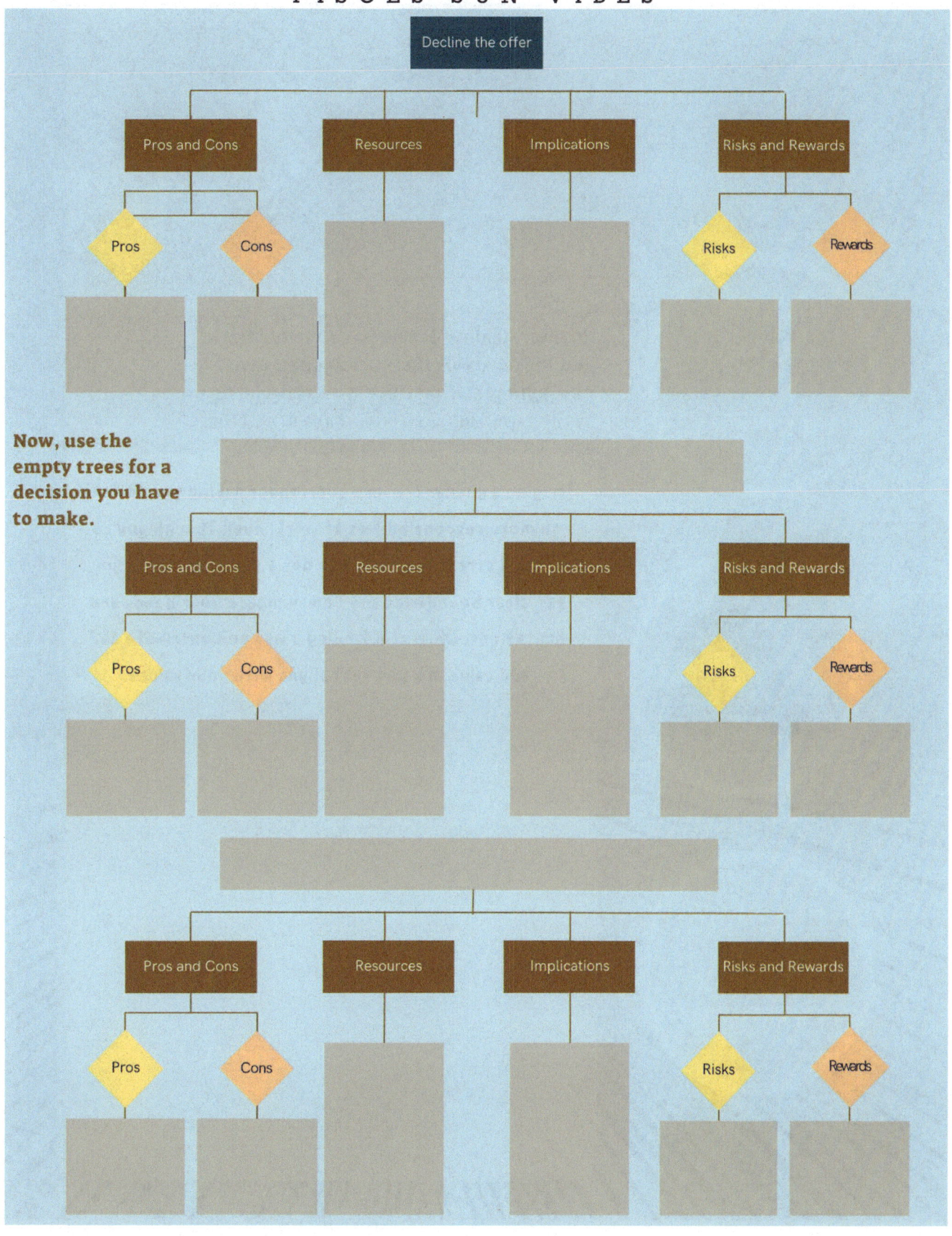

Decline the offer

- Pros and Cons
  - Pros
  - Cons
- Resources
- Implications
- Risks and Rewards
  - Risks
  - Rewards

Now, use the empty trees for a decision you have to make.

- Pros and Cons
  - Pros
  - Cons
- Resources
- Implications
- Risks and Rewards
  - Risks
  - Rewards

- Pros and Cons
  - Pros
  - Cons
- Resources
- Implications
- Risks and Rewards
  - Risks
  - Rewards

49

Pisces

Shadow Energy: SELF-SACRIFICING

In their shadow, Pisces have a tendency to put the needs of others before their own to the point of self-sacrifice. This can lead to feeling used or taken advantage of by others.

Practice: PERSONAL BOUNDARIES

> Imagine a scenario where someone is asking you to take on more responsibilities at work, even though you're already stretched thin. Act out a scenario where you set clear boundaries and communicate your needs and limitations, while still finding a way to contribute and add value in a way that aligns with your values.

DEFINE YOUR BOUNDARIES

Personal boundaries are limits and guidelines that a person sets for themselves in order to establish a healthy sense of self-respect, self-worth, and self-care. By establishing boundaries, individuals can communicate their needs, desires, and limits to others in a clear and respectful manner and create a sense of safety and trust in their relationships.

PHYSICAL
These include personal space and physical touch. Personal physical boundaries can vary from person to person and culture to culture. Some people may be comfortable with close physical proximity and touch, while others may prefer more space and less touch.

EMOTIONAL
These include feelings, thoughts, and opinions. Emotional boundaries involve being clear about what is and isn't acceptable to you in terms of how others treat you emotionally. For example, you may not want to discuss certain personal topics or emotions with certain people.

INTELLECTUAL
These include your thoughts, ideas, and intellectual property. Intellectual boundaries involve protecting your ideas, concepts, and creations from being stolen or used without your permission.

MATERIAL
These include your possessions, time, and money. Material boundaries involve protecting your possessions, finances, and resources from being taken or used without your permission.

TIME
These include the time you spend on various activities and commitments. Time boundaries involve being clear about what is and isn't acceptable to you in terms of how you spend your time and energy, and being willing to say no to commitments that don't align with your priorities or values.

COMMUNICATING YOUR BOUNDARIES

- Identify your boundaries.
- Use "I" statements.
- Be specific and clear.
- Communicate your boundaries early and often.
- Listen to others.
- Be firm and consistent.
- Avoid blaming or shaming.
- Express appreciation when your boundaries are respected.
- Seek support, if needed.

Write the type of boundary.

A person may not want to share intimate or personal information with coworkers or acquaintances.

A person may prefer to keep certain personal ideas or concepts private.

A person may not want to be responsible for paying for other people's expenses or debts.

A person may feel uncomfortable being in a crowded room or a small, confined space.

A person may not want to be around people who are frequently negative or critical.

A person may not want to lend their personal belongings, such as their car or phone, to others.

A person may not want to take on additional work or commitments that interfere with their existing responsibilities or priorities.

A person may prefer not to be hugged or touched by strangers or acquaintances.

A person may prefer to have certain days or times free for personal activities or relaxation.

A person may not want their work or ideas to be used without their permission or without proper credit.

Write 2 boundaries that you have for each category.

PHYSICAL

EMOTIONAL

INTELLECTUAL

MATERIAL

TIME

Personal boundaries are an ongoing process that require reflection, communication, and enforcement. By developing and maintaining healthy boundaries, you can build stronger relationships, protect your well-being, and lead a more fulfilling life.

PISCES SUN VIBES

FRIENDSHIP

With Pisces Sun in friendships, individuals may be highly empathetic, compassionate, and supportive of their friends. They may have a deep sensitivity to others' emotions and may be drawn to friends who share their values or have a spiritual or artistic orientation. However, they may also struggle with people-pleasing or boundary issues in their friendships and may need to develop greater self-awareness and assertiveness to maintain healthy relationships.

SCHOOL

With Pisces Sun in school, individuals may be highly imaginative, creative and intuitive and find fulfillment in artistic or spiritual pursuits. They could have a strong empathy for others and be drawn to service or social justice work. However, they may struggle with practical matters such as organization or discipline, and need extra support and guidance to develop these skills.

CAREER

With Pisces Sun in career, individuals may be highly creative, compassionate and service-oriented, and find fulfillment in careers that allow them to use their gifts to uplift others. They may have a deep connection to the spiritual or mystical realms and be drawn to artistic or healing professions. However, they could also struggle with setting boundaries between their public and private life, and need to cultivate greater focus and ambition to succeed in their careers.

FINANCES

With Pisces Sun in money and finance, individuals may have a complicated relationship with money and struggle with practical matters such as budgeting and financial planning. They could be drawn to spiritual or mystical approaches to money, and be prone to escapism or addictive tendencies in response to financial stress. However, they may also have a deep empathy for others and be drawn to using their financial resources to help those in need. They could benefit from cultivating greater self-awareness and discipline in their financial habits.

Write about a time when you overcame a difficult academic challenge. What did you learn from the experience, and how did it help you grow as a person?

Create a mindfulness-based budget that aligns with your values and long-term financial goals.

Make a list of the qualities you look for in a friend. Then, make a list of the qualities you offer as a friend. Compare the two lists.

Reflect on your current job or career path. What do you enjoy about your work, and what are some areas where you feel you could improve?

PISCES SUN VIBES

Sun energy and shadow energy are different levels (high or low) of expression of the natural energy in your energy profile. The expression of your sun energy is aligned with your authentic self. Shadow energy, on the other hand, can be expressed when we are under stress or feel threatened. By recognizing and releasing low vibrational behavior, we can free ourselves from limiting beliefs, negative emotions, and self-defeating patterns, and open ourselves up to new possibilities, experiences, and ways of being by transmuting the shadow energy into sun energy.

ENERGY FREQUENCY

Write each energy trait in the correct box. Which are the high expression and the low expression of the same energy?

transmute: change in nature

In order to transmute our shadow energy, it is helpful to identify the situations, beliefs, and triggers that activate it, as well as the emotions and needs that underlie it. This can involve practices such as mindfulness, journaling, and self-reflection. By identifying and replacing negative patterns that are holding us back, we convert them into more positive, life-affirming ones. Overall, the process of transmuting shadow energy into sun energy is an ongoing one that requires self-awareness, self-compassion, and intentional effort. By recognizing and transforming our shadow energy, we can develop a deeper understanding of ourselves, increase our self-awareness, and cultivate greater fulfillment, purpose, and joy in our lives.

HIGH

escapist   empathetic
intuitive   creative   self-sacrificing
overly sensitive   generous   indecisive
adaptable   naive

LOW

Creative

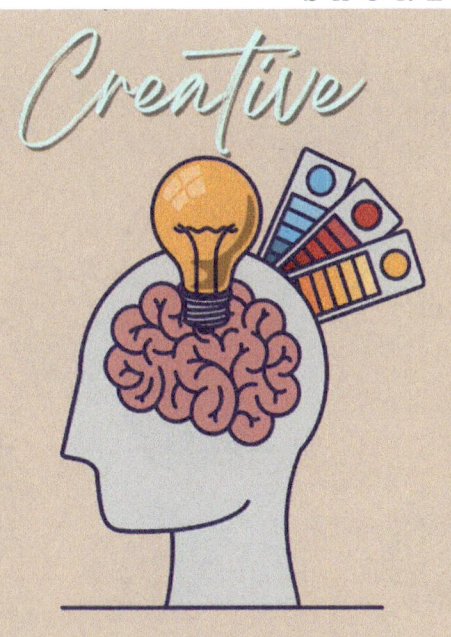

Imagination, innovation, and originality

Expression of mental energy outward

Indecisive

1. Difficulty in making decisions and struggling with committing to a particular course of action

2. Reluctance to express mental energy outward

> "I trust my instincts and have confidence in my ability to make good decisions."

Problem Solving

PISCES SUN VIBES

What are some ways you can channel your moods and emotions into creative projects?

What steps can you take to make decisions more confidently and trust your intuition?

Empathetic

- Understanding and sharing the feelings of others

- Heightened emotions directed outward allowing you to pick up on emotions of others

VS

Naïve

- Tendency to believe or trust others too easily

- Acting from emotion without using discernment

Practice saying "no" to requests or demands that don't align with your values or boundaries, as a way to practice setting healthy limits.

CONCERN FOR OTHERS

PISCES SUN VIBES

> I am discerning and wise, able to distinguish between true generosity and being taken advantage of.

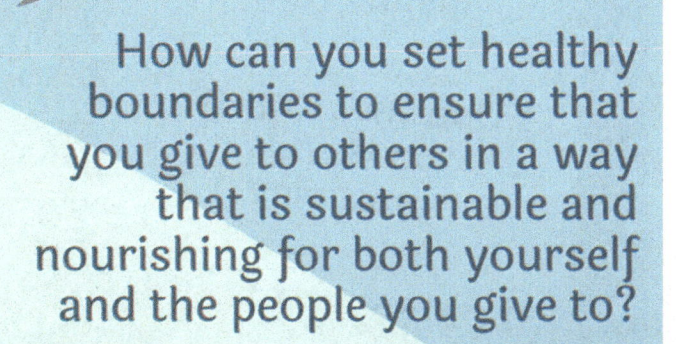

How can you set healthy boundaries to ensure that you give to others in a way that is sustainable and nourishing for both yourself and the people you give to?

EMOTIONAL PROCESSING

Intuitive

Ability to understand something instinctively

Does not require conscious reasoning

VS

Escapist

Tendency to avoid or withdraw from reality

Seeks refuge in imagination or through various forms of distraction

I trust my intuition to guide me towards the right path in life.

How can you better balance your need for imagination and escape with your need to be present in the here and now?

Spend time engaging in a creative activity or immersing yourself in a good book, but set a time limit or schedule to ensure that you don't retreat for too long.

Interaction with Others
Generous vs Overly Sensitive

Generous
- Willingness to give to others
- Giving positive energy to others

> I am a generous and giving person, but I also value and respect my own needs and boundaries.

Overly Sensitive
- Tendency to be easily hurt or affected by criticism or negativity
- Internalizing negative energy

PISCES SUN VIBES

Reflect on a situation where you successfully navigated a challenge by trusting in yourself and not being overly influenced by external factors or opinions. How did your confidence impact the outcome, and what strategies can you apply in the future to maintain this balance?

Practice self-care activities, such as meditation or spending time in nature, as a way to nurture your sensitive side and recharge your emotional batteries.

ADAPTABLE

Ability to adjust to new situations

Flexible and able to navigate change

Tendency to put the needs of others before one's own

Prioritize the needs of others over their own well-being

SELF SACRIFICING

Practice setting clear boundaries and prioritizing self-care, even during times of change or transition.

RESPONSE TO OTHERS' NEEDS

PISCES SUN VIBES

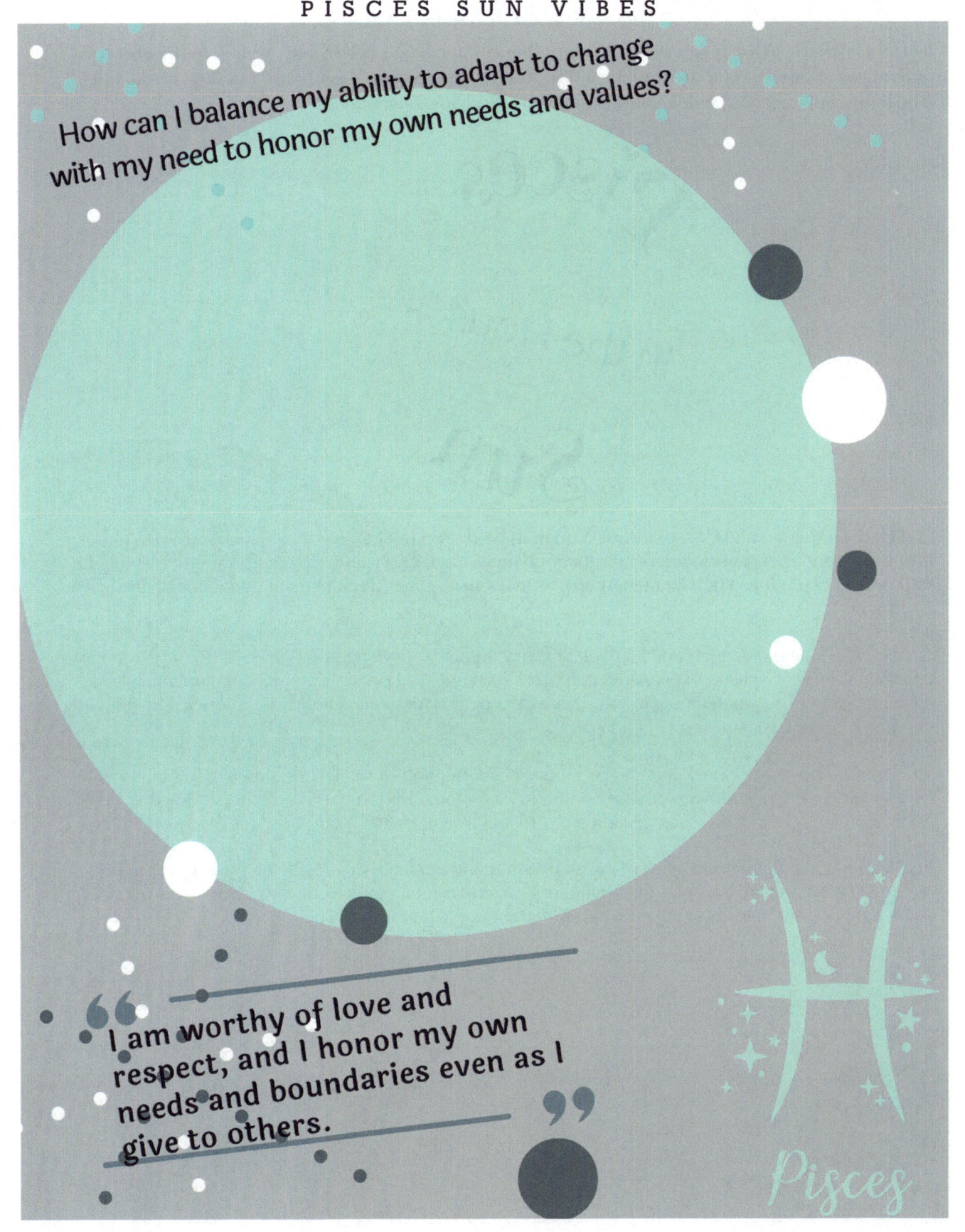

How can I balance my ability to adapt to change with my need to honor my own needs and values?

"I am worthy of love and respect, and I honor my own needs and boundaries even as I give to others."

Pisces

Pisces Sun In the Houses

1st House (Self): A very sensitive and empathetic nature, you are highly attuned to the emotions and needs of others, which can make it difficult for you to assert your own needs and identity. You may come across as dreamy, imaginative, and compassionate.

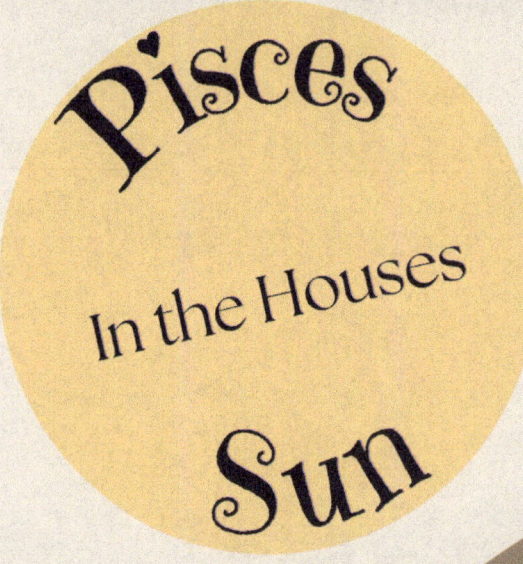

2nd House (Values and Possessions): You may be drawn to creative or mystical pursuits and find fulfillment in expressing yourself through music, art, or writing. However, you may struggle with practical matters such as money or possessions and need to cultivate greater self-discipline and focus.

3rd House (Communication and Immediate Environment): You may be drawn to poetry, literature, or other forms of artistic expression and have a unique and poetic way of communicating your ideas. However, you may struggle with more practical or analytical subjects and need to cultivate greater attention to detail and organization.

4th House (Home and Family): A deep emotional connection to family and home, you may have a strong intuitive sense of what others need and a responsibility to care for others. However, you may also struggle with boundaries and need to learn to prioritize your own needs and self-care.

5th House (Creativity and Self-Expression): A strong creative or artistic streak, you may be highly intuitive and imaginative and have a unique and poetic approach to life. However, you may also struggle with self-doubt or uncertainty about your creative abilities.

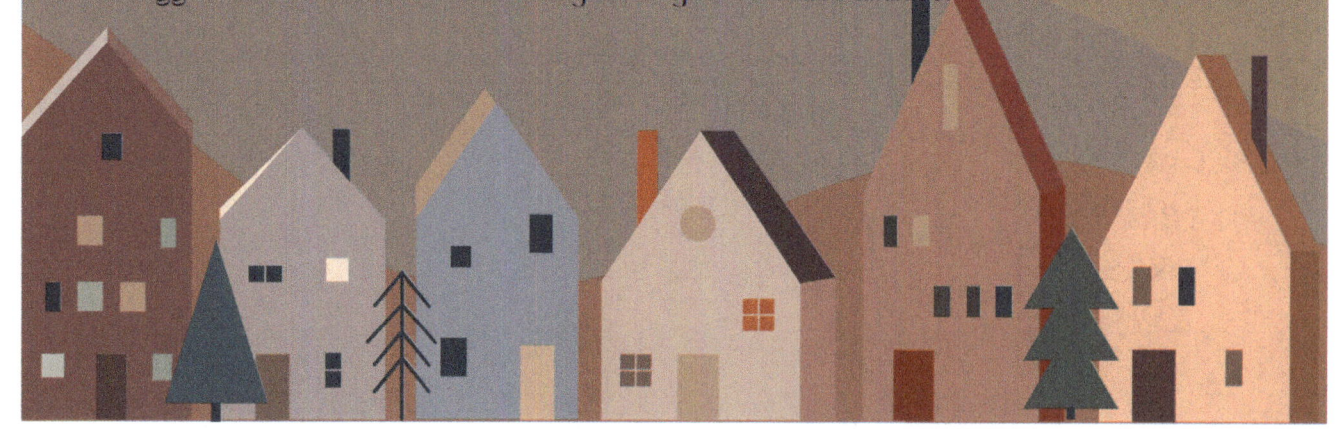

PISCES SUN VIBES

6th House (Work and Health): A strong desire to help others and be drawn to healing or service professions. you may have a deep empathy for others and find fulfillment in using your gifts to support others. However, you may also struggle with self-care and boundaries and need to cultivate greater attention to your own health and well-being.

7th House (Relationships): A strong need for connection. you may be highly intuitive and compassionate and have a deep desire to create harmony and understanding in your relationships. However, you may also struggle with boundaries and need to cultivate greater assertiveness in your relationships.

8th House (Intimacy and Transformation): You may have a deep understanding of the mysteries of life and death and be drawn to transformative experiences. However, you may also struggle with boundaries in your intimate relationships and need to cultivate greater self-awareness and emotional honesty.

9th House (Expansion and Higher Learning): A strong spiritual or philosophical outlook on life. you may be drawn to mystical or esoteric teachings and find fulfillment in pursuing higher learning or travel. However, you may also struggle with practical or mundane matters.

10th House (Career and Public Life): A strong desire to help others and make a positive impact in the world. you may find fulfillment in using your gifts to uplift others. However, you may also struggle with setting boundaries between your public and private life and need to cultivate greater focus and ambition to succeed in your career.

11th House (Community and Networking): You may have a deep empathy for others and find fulfillment in creating community and support systems for those in need. However, you may also struggle with people-pleasing or boundary issues in your friendships and need to cultivate greater self-awareness and assertiveness.

12th House (Subconscious and Hidden Matters): A deep connection to the spiritual or mystical realms. you may have a rich inner world and find fulfillment in exploring your dreams, subconscious, and intuition. However, you may also struggle with boundaries between yourself and others and need to cultivate greater self-awareness and emotional honesty.

Set up a comfortable space with watercolors, paper, and a cup of water.
Close your eyes and take a few deep breaths to center yourself.
Dip your brush in water, then in the paint, and let your emotions guide you as you create fluid, flowing strokes on the paper.
Let go of any expectations and allow your creativity to flow freely like water.
Continue for 10-15 minutes or until you feel satisfied with your creation.

Find a quiet, comfortable place to sit or lie down.
Close your eyes and take slow, deep breaths, focusing on the sound of your breath.
Imagine the sound of your breath as waves crashing on the shore, bringing calm and serenity.
Allow any thoughts or distractions to wash away with the waves.
Continue for 5-10 minutes, then gently return to the present moment.

Flowing Art
Stimulates the flow of energy

Ocean Breathing Meditation
Calms the mind and balances the flow of energy

Water Cleansing Ritual
Removes negative energy

Emotional Shield Visualization
Promotes a sense of safety and security

Creative · Mindfulness · Cleansing · Protecting

Prepare a bowl of water, adding a pinch of sea salt or a few drops of essential oil if desired.
Find a quiet space and sit comfortably with the bowl in front of you.
Close your eyes and take a few deep breaths to center yourself.
Dip your fingers in the water and gently sprinkle it on your face, arms, and any other areas where you feel the need for cleansing.
As you do this, visualize the water washing away any negative energy or emotions.
When you're finished, dispose of the water outside, returning it to the earth.

Find a quiet, comfortable place to sit or stand.
Close your eyes and take a few deep breaths to center yourself.
Visualize a sphere of water energy surrounding you, like a protective shield.
Imagine the shield as a barrier that repels negative emotions and energy, keeping you safe and balanced.
Hold this visualization for 5-10 minutes, then gently release it and return to the present moment.

PISCES SUN VIBES

HEALING *Nature*

Stress Relief | **Mental Clarity** | **Enhance Creativity** | **Connect with Spiritual Energy**

Spend some time in nature, such as by taking a walk in the woods or sitting by a river, to tap into your natural sense of intuition and connection to the world around you.

> Immersing myself in nature, I embrace the flow of life, finding healing, tranquility, and a deeper connection to the universe.

SHONETTE CHARLES

Vacation Trip

Spiritual or Wellness

HOW CAN YOU DESIGN VACATIONS THAT CATER TO YOUR NATURAL ENERGY NEEDS AND ALLOW YOU TO RECHARGE AND RENEW?

Beach

Coastal Road Trip

- ✓ Deepen Spirituality
- ✓ Water
- ✓ Help Others

Volunteer Vacation

Cruise

VACATIONS CAN BE A CHANCE TO EXPERIENCE DIFFERENT ENERGIES AND APPROACHES. HOW MIGHT EMBRACING NEW ENERGIES EXPAND YOUR HORIZONS AND BRING FRESH PERSPECTIVES?

Pisces Through the Planets

PISCES SUN VIBES

Pisces Suns are highly intuitive, sensitive, and empathetic, with a deep connection to the spiritual or mystical realms.

Pisces Moon's emotions are deeply influenced by their intuition and imagination, and they may be prone to strong moods or emotional highs and lows.

Pisces Mercury's communication style is highly intuitive and imaginative, and they may have a poetic or artistic way of expressing themselves.

Pisces Saturn's sense of responsibility and structure is highly influenced by their emotional boundaries and intuition, and they may struggle with practical matters or self-discipline.

Pisces Neptune has a deep connection to the spiritual or mystical realms, and may be drawn to creative or metaphysical pursuits. They may also struggle with boundaries between reality and fantasy or may be prone to escapism or addiction.

Pisces Risings are dreamy, imaginative, and empathetic, with a gentle and compassionate demeanor.

Pisces Plutos' sense of transformation and power is highly influenced by their emotional boundaries and intuition, and they may have a deep desire to heal or transform others through spiritual or mystical means.

Pisces Venus values love, beauty, and harmony, and may be drawn to artistic or spiritual pursuits in their relationships and creative pursuits.

Pisces Jupiter's sense of growth and expansion is highly influenced by their spiritual or metaphysical beliefs, and they may find fulfillment in pursuing mystical or esoteric knowledge.

Pisces Mars' drive and energy are highly influenced by their intuition and imagination, and they may be drawn to creative or spiritual pursuits in their actions and

Pisces Uranus' sense of innovation and change is highly influenced by their imagination and intuition, and they may be drawn to unconventional or artistic

SHONETTE CHARLES

8 Pisces HOBBIES

What strategies are you most eager to apply to help you transmute shadow energy?

1. Meditation

2. Volunteering

3. Spirituality

4. Drawing or Painting

How have the insights in this journal shifted your perspective about your strengths, challenges, and approach to life?

5. Playing an Instrument

6. Singing

7. Swimming

How will understanding your sun sign energy better contribute to your future growth and success?

8. Dancing

Consider how engaging in these activities allows you to channel your natural energy.

72

Made in the USA
Columbia, SC
27 June 2023